25.49

W9-BNQ-292

Three Blue Pigeons

Retold by NICHOLAS IAN
Illustrations by SUSAN REAGAN
Music by MARK OBLINGER

CANTATA
LEARNING

WWW.CANTATALEARNING.COM

CANTATA LEARNING

Published by Cantata Learning
1710 Roe Crest Drive
North Mankato, MN 56003
www.cantatalearning.com

A note to educators and librarians from the publisher: Cantata Learning has provided the following data to assist in book processing and suggested use of Cantata Learning product.

Publisher's Cataloging-in-Publication Data
Prepared by Librarian Consultant: Ann-Marie Begnaud
Library of Congress Control Number: 2016938100
    Three Blue Pigeons
    Series: Sing-along Songs : Math
    Retold by Nicholas Ian
    Illustrations by Susan Reagan
    Music by Mark Oblinger
    Summary: Simple subtraction and addition are made easy in this twist on the classic song Three Blue Pigeons.
    ISBN: 978-1-63290-801-8 (library binding/CD)
Suggested Dewey and Subject Headings:
    Dewey: E 513.21
    LCSH Subject Headings: Mathematics – Juvenile literature. | Mathematics – Songs and music – Texts. | Mathematics – Juvenile sound recordings.
    Sears Subject Headings: Addition. | Subtraction. | Mathematics. | School songbooks. | Children's songs. | Folk music – United States.
    BISAC Subject Headings: JUVENILE NONFICTION / Mathematics / Arithmetic. | JUVENILE NONFICTION / Music / Songbooks. | JUVENILE NONFICTION / Concepts / Counting & Numbers.

Book design and art direction: Tim Palin Creative
Editorial direction: Flat Sole Studio
Music direction: Elizabeth Draper
Music written and produced by Mark Oblinger

Printed in the United States of America in North Mankato, Minnesota.
122016   0339CGS17

ACCESS THE MUSIC!

SCAN CODE WITH MOBILE APP

CANTATALEARNING.COM

TIPS TO SUPPORT LITERACY AT HOME

WHY READING AND SINGING WITH YOUR CHILD IS SO IMPORTANT

Daily reading with your child leads to increased academic achievement. Music and songs, specifically rhyming songs, are a fun and easy way to build early literacy and language development. Music skills correlate significantly with both phonological awareness and reading development. Singing helps build vocabulary and speech development. And reading and appreciating music together is a wonderful way to strengthen your relationship.

READ AND SING EVERY DAY!

TIPS FOR USING CANTATA LEARNING BOOKS AND SONGS DURING YOUR DAILY STORY TIME

1. As you sing and read, point out the different words on the page that rhyme. Suggest other words that rhyme.

2. Memorize simple rhymes such as Itsy Bitsy Spider and sing them together. This encourages comprehension skills and early literacy skills.

3. Use the questions in the back of each book to guide your singing and storytelling.

4. Read the included sheet music with your child while you listen to the song. How do the music notes correlate to the words of the song?

5. Sing along on the go and at home. Access music by scanning the QR code on each Cantata book, or by using the included CD. You can also stream or download the music for free to your computer, smartphone, or mobile device.

Devoting time to daily reading shows that you are available for your child. Together, you are building language, literacy, and listening skills.

Have fun reading and singing!

Pigeons live almost everywhere. In the city, you might find them in a park. In the country, they might **roost** in a barn. You can use pigeons to help you learn **addition** and **subtraction**. When a pigeon flies away, subtract one. When one flies back, add one.

Now turn the page and count the pigeons. Remember to sing along!

5

Three blue pigeons sitting on the wall.
Three blue pigeons sitting on the wall.

The first one flew away.
Whee!

Two blue pigeons sitting on the wall.

Two blue pigeons sitting on the wall.

8

The second one flew away.
Whee!

One blue pigeon sitting on the wall.
One blue pigeon sitting on the wall.

10

The third one flew away.
Whee!

No blue pigeons sitting on the wall.

No blue pigeons sitting on the wall.

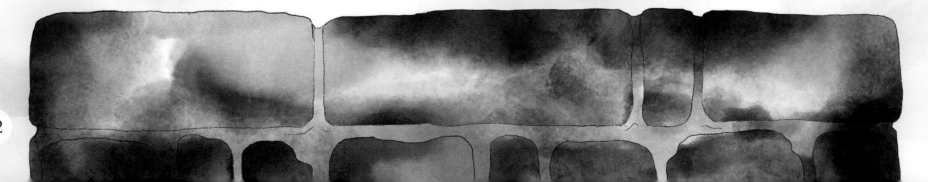

The first one flew back.
Whee!

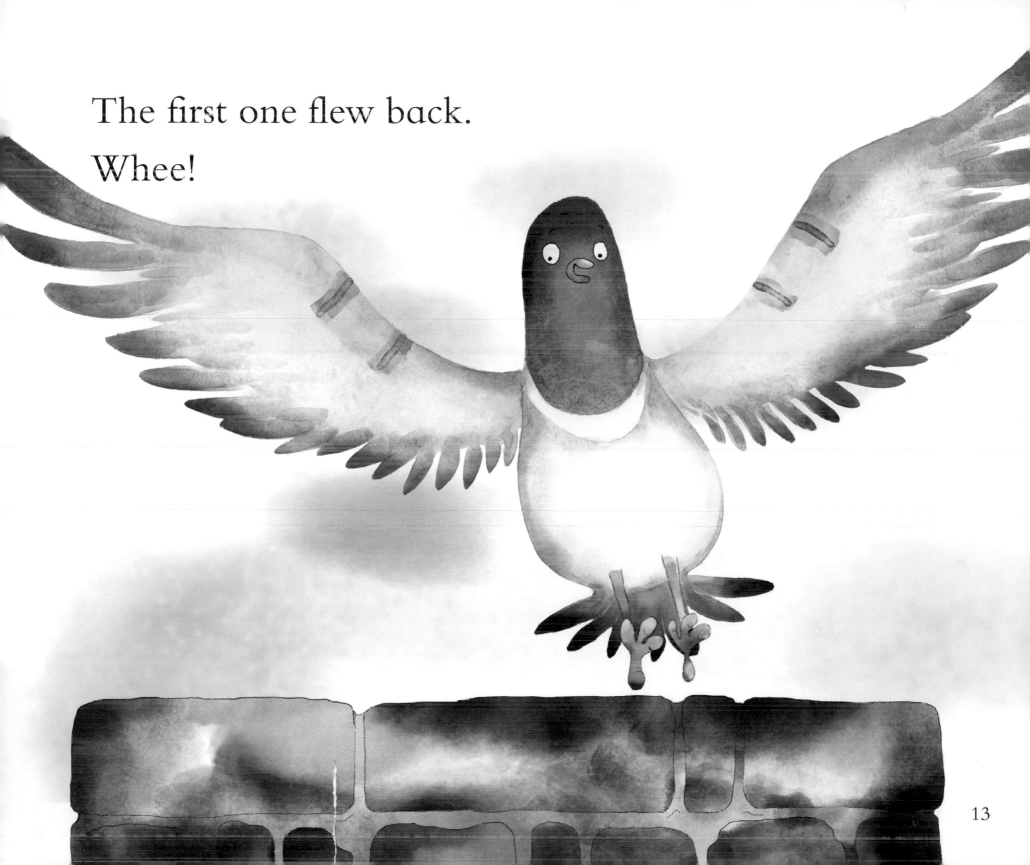

One blue pigeon sitting on the wall.

One blue pigeon sitting on the wall.

14

The second one flew back.
Whee!

Two blue pigeons sitting on the wall.
Two blue pigeons sitting on the wall.

16

The third one flew back.
Whee!

17

Three blue pigeons sitting on the wall.
Three blue pigeons sitting on the wall.

The pigeons are all home!
Whee!

18

Three blue pigeons sitting on the wall.

Three blue pigeons sitting on the wall.

The pigeons are all home!

One! Two! Three!

SONG LYRICS
Three Blue Pigeons

Three blue pigeons sitting
on the wall.
Three blue pigeons sitting
on the wall.

The first one flew away.
Whee!

Two blue pigeons sitting on
the wall.
Two blue pigeons sitting on
the wall.

The second one flew away.
Whee!

One blue pigeon sitting on
the wall.
One blue pigeon sitting on
the wall.

The third one flew away.
Whee!

No blue pigeons sitting on
the wall.
No blue pigeons sitting on
the wall.

The first one flew back.
Whee!

One blue pigeon sitting on
the wall.
One blue pigeon sitting on
the wall.

The second one flew back.
Whee!

Two blue pigeons sitting on
the wall.
Two blue pigeons sitting on
the wall.

The third one flew back.
Whee!

Three blue pigeons sitting
on the wall.
Three blue pigeons sitting
on the wall.

The pigeons are all home!
Whee!

Three blue pigeons sitting
on the wall.
Three blue pigeons sitting
on the wall.

The pigeons are all home!
One! Two! Three!

22

Three Blue Pigeons

Americana
Mark Oblinger

Verse

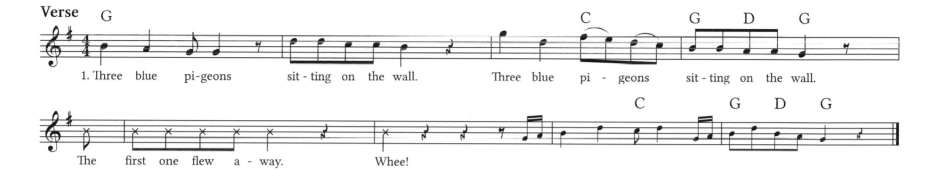

1. Three blue pi-geons sit-ting on the wall. Three blue pi-geons sit-ting on the wall.

The first one flew a-way. Whee!

Verse 2
Two blue pigeons sitting on the wall.
Two blue pigeons sitting on the wall.
The second one flew away.
Whee!

Verse 3
One blue pigeon sitting on the wall.
One blue pigeon sitting on the wall.
The third one flew away.
Whee!

Verse 4
No blue pigeons sitting on the wall.
No blue pigeons sitting on the wall.
The first one flew back.
Whee!

Verse 5
One blue pigeon sitting on the wall.
One blue pigeon sitting on the wall.
The second one flew back.
Whee!

Verse 6
Two blue pigeons sitting on the wall.
Two blue pigeons sitting on the wall.
The third one flew back.
Whee!

Verse 7
Three blue pigeons sitting on the wall.
Three blue pigeons sitting on the wall.
The pigeons are all home!
Whee!

Outro

Three blue pi-geons sit-ting on the wall. Three blue pi-geons sit-ting on the wall. The pi-geons are all home! One! Two! Three!

GLOSSARY

addition—the act of adding numbers

roost—a place where birds sleep

subtraction—the act of taking away one number from another

GUIDED READING ACTIVITIES

1. The girl in the book counts pigeons, but there are many things to count. Look around your room. How many books do you have?

2. What do you get if you take one away from three? How about when you subtract two from three? Now subtract three from three. What is left?

3. Draw your favorite animal. Now draw another animal next to it. And another. How many animals have you drawn?

TO LEARN MORE

Penn, M. W. *It's Subtraction*. North Mankato, MN: Capstone, 2012.

Rissman, Rebecca. *Counting at the Park*. North Mankato, MN: Heinemann-Raintree, 2013.

Steffora, Tracey. *Adding with Ants*. North Mankato, MN: Heinemann-Raintree, 2014.

Steffora, Tracey. *Taking Away with Tigers*. North Mankato, MN: Heinemann-Raintree, 2014.